Written by **Emily King**   Illustrated by **Ed Olson**

To Adrieanna
& Alix,
Blessings!
Emily King

Clopper

the Christmas Donkey

In honor of
our Savior, the Holy One
once cradled in a manger,
now treasured in our hearts

and to
my mother
who abides in His grace.

Clopper the Christmas Donkey

Text © 2003 by Emily King
Art © 2003 by Ed Olson

Published by Kregel Publications, P.O. Box 2607, Grand Rapids, MI 49501.

Scripture quotations are found in Luke 2:1–20 and are from the *Holy Bible, New International Version*®.
© 1973, 1978, 1984 by International Bible Society. Used by permission of Zondervan Publishing House.
All rights reserved.

Printed in China

ISBN 0-8254-3069-0

My name is Clopper. Nuzzle up while I tell you about a very special night!

It all began early one morning as I was munching on a breakfast of sweet grass. My master, Joseph, came from the house carrying my bridle and sacks of supplies for a journey.

In those days Caesar Augustus issued a decree that a census should be taken of the entire Roman world. . . . And everyone went to his own town to register.

Hee-haw! An adventure!

Joseph helped his wife, Mary, up onto my back. I thought she felt heavier than the last time I carried her.

So Joseph also went up from the town of Nazareth in Galilee to Judea, to Bethlehem the town of David, because he belonged to the house and line of David. He went there to register with Mary, who was pledged to be married to him and was expecting a child.

The road took us over steep, rocky hills and into cool, green valleys. We passed through quiet villages and busy towns.

At last we arrived in Bethlehem. The city buzzed with people who came from near and far.
"Hee-haw. Haw-hee," brayed other donkeys.
Children whipped around us in a game of tag. Mamas scolded. Old friends laughed and shouted and patted each other on the back.

"Joseph," said Mary, "look at all the people who have come to Bethlehem."
"Yes," Joseph sighed. "It will not be easy to find a room."

We trudged through town, along streets, down dusty paths. Joseph knocked on door after door. No one had an empty room. The sky darkened and the air grew colder. I smelled simmering stew and fresh-baked bread. My tummy growled like a hungry lion and my hooves ached up to my knees!

"I can see you are weary," Joseph told Mary.

Mary smiled. "The Lord will provide a place for us to stay. I know He will."

Finally, Joseph found a kind innkeeper. At first the innkeeper shook his head and said, "I'm very sorry. I have no room for you in the inn."

Then he looked at Mary. "It is late and you are both tired. You are welcome to stay in my stable. It is not much, but at least you will be able to get some rest."

Joseph took the heavy bags from my back. *Hee-haw!* What a relief! And there was crunchy hay and fresh water for supper.

Mary and Joseph didn't usually sleep with cows or sheep . . . or even donkeys. But they stretched out on a bed of straw and rested.

I nodded off to sleep, too. Then I heard it.

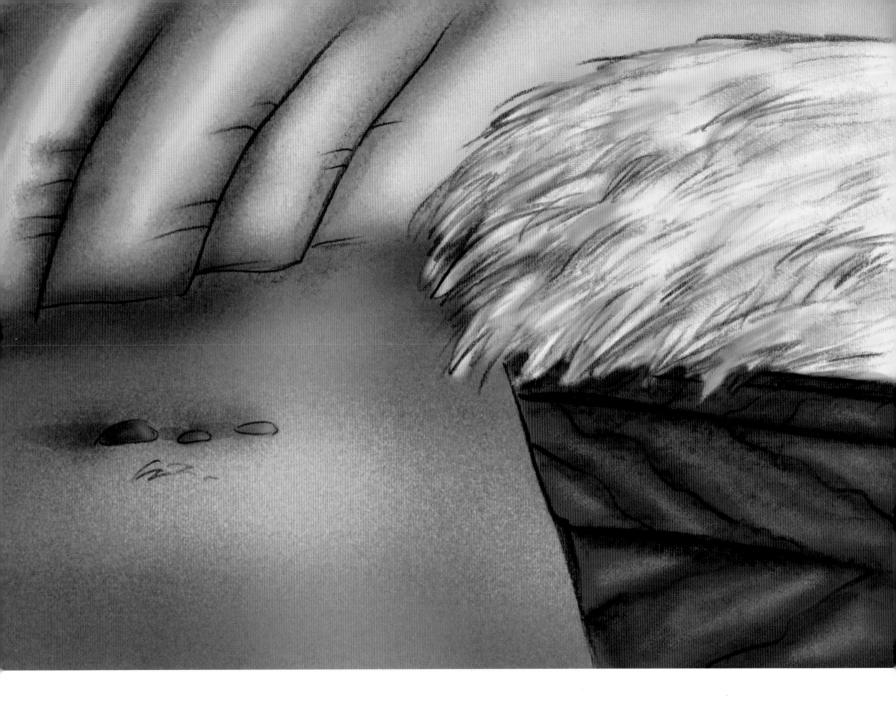

The sound of a . . . a . . .

. . . a BABY! Mary had given birth to a baby boy! Baby Jesus. They wrapped Him in cloths and laid Him in the manger. That is where we animals eat our hay. I clip-clopped over to where He lay. What a sweet little child! I could tell He was very special.

While they were there, the time came for the baby to be born, and she gave birth to her firstborn, a son. She wrapped him in cloths and placed him in a manger, because there was no room for them in the inn.

Near Him, I felt as peaceful as a sleeping lamb, from the tip of my nose to the swish of my tail. Mary and Joseph kissed His rosy cheeks, and sang soft and beautiful praise songs.

I fell asleep again. Then excited voices jolted me awake. One shepherd called to the others, "Here! I have found the Christ child!" The shepherds rushed into the stable. The tall one and short one bumped into the first one when he stopped.

"May we see Him?" they asked.
"Of course. Come in," Joseph answered softly.
"Shhhh," the chubby one whispered as they tiptoed to the manger.

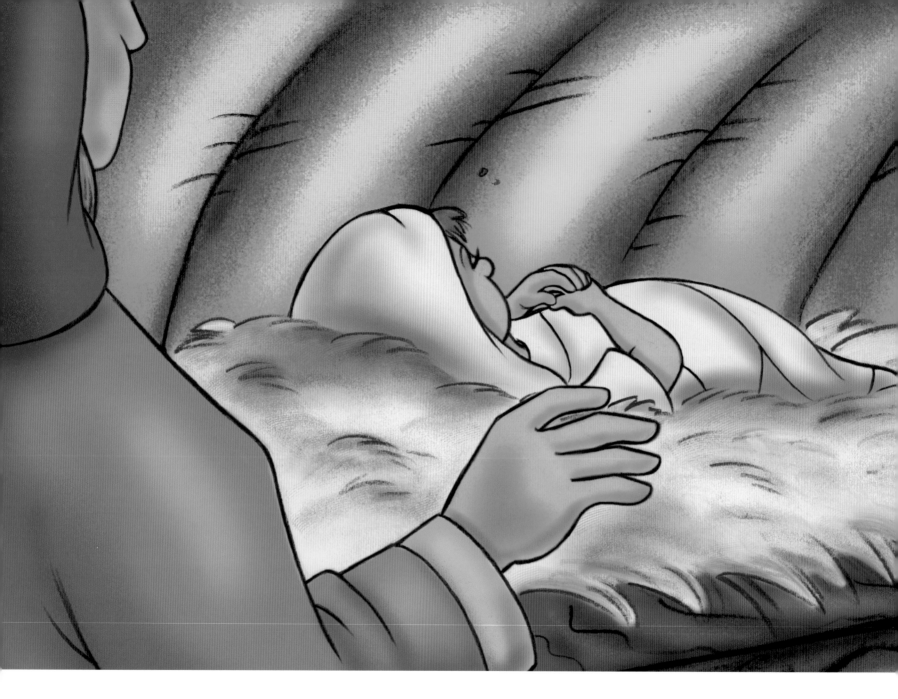

They dropped to their knees by the manger. As quiet and still as statues, they gazed at baby Jesus.

Then the tall shepherd spoke. "We were watching our sheep," he said, "when an angel suddenly appeared and surrounded us with bright light."

"Yes," said the short one, "we shook in our sandals, but he told us not to be afraid."

And there were shepherds living out in the fields nearby, keeping watch over their flocks at night. An angel of the Lord appeared to them, and the glory of the Lord shone around them, and they were terrified. But the angel said to them, "Do not be afraid. I bring you good news of great joy that will be for all the people. Today in the town of David a Savior has been born to you; he is Christ the Lord. This will be a sign to you: You will find a baby wrapped in cloths and lying in a manger."

The angel said, "I bring you good news which will bring joy to many people."

Suddenly a great company of the heavenly host appeared with the angel, praising God and saying, "Glory to God in the highest, and on earth peace to men on whom his favor rests." When the angels had left them and gone into heaven, the shepherds said to one another, "Let's go to Bethlehem and see this thing that has happened, which the Lord has told us about."

The other shepherd spoke up, "And then, you wouldn't believe what we saw. The sky was filled with light! Hundreds . . . no, thousands . . . of angels sang,

'Glory to God in the highest and on Earth, peace and goodwill to men.'"

The tall shepherd said, "God has kept His promise to send us a Savior." Mary and Joseph's eyes twinkled as they listened.

When they had seen him, they spread the word concerning what had been told them about this child, and all who heard it were amazed at what the shepherds said to them.

"Yes," Mary said with a nod, "the Lord has truly blessed us with this child."
"Let's hurry home and tell our families," said the other shepherd.

I wonder if people believed the shepherds. Well, whether others believed their story or not, I know it's true. I saw it with my own eyes. I was there that special night when Mary gave birth to baby Jesus . . .

But Mary treasured up all these things and pondered them in her heart. The shepherds returned, glorifying and praising God for all the things they had heard and seen, which were just as they had been told.

. . . the Lord Jesus, the Savior of the world.